Banging Your Way

How to Pick-up, Flirt, Seduce, and Sleep with Women on Craigslist

Copyright © 2014 by Braun Schweiger

Table of Contents

Before you get started 3

Why you need to read this 5

Getting started 8

A Tale of Two Ads 11

Posting your first ad 18

Responding to an ad 24

Sample ads 40

Final wrap up 52

Before you get started

Bang*ing Your Way Across Craigslist* is all about rebooting your sex life.

You don't have to hang out in smoky bars and clubs anymore; no more cheesy pickup lines; or getting shot down time after time while the guys watch your feeble pickup attempts.

Craigslist opens up an entirely new world of dating for you to explore, but along with great dating comes great responsibility.

There are a few rules of the game you need to honor and obey along the way.

1) No means – No. If you're on a date and she tells you no or pushes you away you need to respect her decision.

2) If she is under eighteen get your ass out of there quick-like. If there's ever any doubt play the role of the dubious bartender and check her id.

3) There aren't any second chances in this life. It's up to you to play safe so before you play the game wrap that thing up in a condom – It protects the both of you.

4) Keep an eye on your wallet and your car keys. Craigslist is loaded with scams and scammers. I never bring

more than a few bucks with me when I'm meeting anyone new, and I unload the credit cards in a safe place at home. It limits my losses if something bad happens.

5) Don't walk away from your drinks. This is a warning usually given to women, but it applies to men as well. There's always a chance the girl or an accomplice could slip something into your drink. If you have any doubts pretend you're a little clumsy and knock it on the floor. That way you can order a fresh one.

6) If it doesn't feel right walk away. Gut instincts are usually right on. Make up some crazy story about having to walk the dog or check on your kids and get out of there.

Why you need to read this

The problem most guys have getting laid on Craigslist is they let their dick get in the way of their commonsense.

Why else would you see all those dick picks in dating ads? Read every woman's ad. The first thing they have to say is "don't send me a picture of your thing." "No dick pics!" "Ooh it's gross!"

Guys, I hate to tell you but women are just like you, they want to see a face or body pic. It's their natural defense action at work. They want to make sure you're not super fat, or a one eyed Cyclops, or some sort of psycho killer type.

Second thing I'm here to tell you is most women aren't going to respond to your ad when it's titled "Let's fuck!" "Suck on this." Or "I've got a really big package waiting for you!"

I know there's a guy out there writing dating books and one of his favorite lines is "You know she's a slut when..." and he goes on to list all of these tells, but trust me the only response you're going to get to these ads are pictures from girls with their phone number and business hours posted over it, or girls writing to tell you "You've got to pay to play" or "Donations kindly accepted" or "for generous guys only."

Can you say hookers? Nothing wrong with that if that's the type of girl you want to attract. It's a sure thing. You're going to be out a few hundred bucks, and maybe catch an STD or two. It's entirely your choice.

Women are looking for something a little different. Sure most of them want it as much as you do but they don't like to think of themselves as sluts. They want to have a great date and just sort of have the sex follow naturally if it's meant to happen.

Women are looking for a little finesse and a little romancing. They want the boyfriend experience even if you both know it's just for one night.

So what's a guy to do?

That's what this book is all about.

First, we're going to take a look at the ads most guys post on Craigslist and examine what the hell's wrong with them.

Second, we're going to look at the ads women post on Craigslist and try to figure out what they want.

Finally, we're going to put together a strategy, and develop some sample ads that will help you get what you want as well as help the women who respond to your ads get what they want.

Fair enough?

Getting started

Hey everyone – Braun Scwheiger here. I've spent the last four years banging my way across Craigslist, and I've had some of the most mind blowing sexual experiences ever - eager young girls, older women, and even some pregnant young mommas. The best part about it was ... each and every one of them sent me their pictures, and begged me to go out with them. I didn't have to use a single pick up line, didn't have to hang out in any smoky bars or clubs. I just chilled by my computer scoping out online porn sites and waiting for my email notifications.

Let me tell you about it.

Here's the first ad I ever posted on Craigslist...

Days are getting longer and colder, looking for a soft warm cuddle buddy

Could you be her? I'm looking for a gal to come over, cuddle up close on the couch, watch a few movies, and stay warm by the fire. Nothing too serious, just good talk, fun, and...

Tell me what you want to watch and I'll have snacks and wine waiting for your movie time.

Be sure to include a pic to set yourself apart from the pack, and to get my fastest reply.

All warm and fuzzy, isn't it? That's what girls like. They want to fuck but they don't want to feel like a slut the next morning when it's all done. The cuddle buddy is a soft sell approach that will give your email box a serious workout. Give it a try and get ready for some regular action.

The reason the cuddle buddy / snuggle buddy approach works so well comes down to its very definition. The urban dictionary defines snuggle buddy as:

"...a close friend you sometimes cuddle up with when you feel down or in need of comforting. There's no sex involved and it never goes further than a cuddle."

There's absolutely no expectation going into it. That's what makes the cuddle buddy approach so effective. It sets you up for a night of holding each other tight, cuddled up under the blanket watching TV or a movie. If you approach it that way you may be in for a great night of making out, maybe even sex. If not you still enjoyed a great night cuddled up with a soft sexy lady.

That ad drew thirteen responses three in-person cuddle buddy meet-ups, and two nights of mind blowing sex.

Not every ad is going to be that successful. Don't worry if one ad doesn't hit a home run; it's all part of the game. Some ads draw a lot of responses, some draw a complete blank. I have three or four personal ads running every day. I consider Craigslist to be something like my own personal research laboratory. I work with about fifteen basic ads and I'm constantly tweaking them for maximum effect. You'd be surprised the difference switching out one or two words can make.

A Tale of Two Ads

Here's the ad a typical guy posts on Craigslist.

Big tits a must

Average guy looking for freaky lady with big tits to blow me, fuck me, and let me shoot a load all over your face and tits. Prefer a squirter.

Pics a must, I want to see those titties before we jump into anything. You should host or spring for a motel room.

It's right to the point – fuck/suck, and it goes without saying he posted one or two big dick pics. If this is the kind of ad you're thinking about posting it's going to be a really tough sell to get any women to respond.

You're telling her all you want is sex.

More than that, you're putting it all on her. You're asking her to do special requests, and then you tell her – oh, by-the-way, send me some pics so I can make sure you're not some ugly fat loser bitch. Then to make it worse yet the majority of guys ask her to host (because they have a wife or girlfriend at home they don't want to know about their clandestine encounter).

Think about it from her perspective. There are all sorts of stories out there about the Craigslist Killer, and psycho's who stalk women on Craigslist.

Your ad is asking her to disregard all of these danger signs and invite you into her home for a sexual rendezvous without ever meeting with you first.

Sorry to tell you dude, but you've got a better chance of winning the lottery.

———————

Here's a less threatening approach that will bring you a lot more responses, and help to disarm her natural defenses.

Meet for dinner and a drink, see if anything sparks

Sane, good looking businessman, with construction worker build, is looking to take a lady out for dinner and drinks tonight. My thought is we could watch a little football on the big screen, swap a few stories, and maybe even make fun of the guys hitting on girls by the bar.

Who knows if something sparks between us we might even head back to my place to close the night out.

No need for a picture right off, we can email back and forth a few times first, and if you're comfortable then we could text each other pictures and pick a place to meet up.

Hit me up if you're interested.

_____

What do you think?

Ad number one drew three replies. One lady sent a few sexy pics and a note that said you've "got to pay to play." The other two responses were from the professionals – topless photos with their email and phone # across the picture.

The second ad drew replies from those same three hooker bots, but it also received seven real responses. I emailed back and forth several times with three of them, set two dates, and had a great time.

What's the big difference?

The second ad is less threatening. It doesn't say anything about sex, or blow jobs, or spurting cum all over her body; although some of it is subtly implied when you say, *"Who knows, if something sparks between us, we might even head back to my place to close the night out."*

The other thing you should notice is it's very casual and conversational; dinner and drinks, TV and talk, making fun of the lame ass drunks picking up chicks at the bar. It pokes fun at your own situation and lets you turn the tables on it.

Finally, it's not pushy. There's no need for pictures right off, let's email back and forth a little first, then we can text pictures to each other when you feel comfortable.

The entire ad plays into a woman's mindset – safety; sexy, but non-threatening; not just looking to get into her panties.

Here's a similar ad I just ran, and one of the conversations that developed out of it.

Burger Basket Night at the Last Round Up

Monday night is Burger Basket Night at the Last Round Up. Any gals want to meet up there for good food, conversation, and see if any chemistry sparks where we might want to do it again. I'm a pretty regular guy, sane, educated, kids – Looking for a lady with a similar background. You should be between the ages of 35 and 55, prefer taller, don't care if you've got a few extra pounds on you (I do too).

Just to show you I'm a big spender I'll spring for the burger basket ($3.25 including a large ice water).

Get back to me with a few words about yourself. We can email back and forth a few times, discover a little more about each other, and decide if we want to exchange pics or not.

Please be available between 5:00 and 9:00 on Monday. It would be a shame to miss that burger basket.

Again, it's low key, humorous, and doesn't include a single reference about sex. Everything in the ad is designed to bring down a girl's natural defense shields – Dinner in a public place, big spender - $3.25 for a burger basket, no pressure for pictures up front. The whole experience is laid back, talk a little first; then we can decide if we want to swap pics.

Here's one of the better conversations that came out of that one.

Her: "A burger basket. How could a woman turn that down?"

Me: "Do you think it's too much. Maybe we could split an appetizer or desert?"

Her: "Not sure about the desert, but an appetizer would be awesome!"

Me: "Could I recommend the Blooming Onion, or would cheese fries suit you better? What's your favorite dip?"

Her: "Why don't you send me your number, so I can text you a pic. Maybe that will help you pick the dip?"

See how easy it is. Just a few brief lines back and forth, play off the words in the ad and match its tone. It doesn't usually take much to prove you're real, and someone she'd like to get to know.

The key is to match her style. Pace your responses to what she is saying. If she writes something short, send back a short reply.

If she sends you a complete novel describing her life pick up on two or three points that interest you and throw in some details about yourself.

Don't push her for pics or a quick meeting; she's going to let you know when she's comfortable with you. Odds are she'll send you a pic or ask for a few details about what you look like. If she likes what she hears she'll tell you a little bit about herself and ask for your cell number so you can exchange pics. At that point a personal meet-up is right around the corner, assuming neither of you lied about your looks.

Posting your first ad

When you first get started with it Craigslist can seem a little scary, but once you've take a few moments to familiarize yourself with the site it's actually quite easy to navigate and post ads.

Craigslist dating ads can be found under the general heading of Personals. After that they're broken down into nine different categories.

1. Strictly platonic

2. Women seek women

3. Women seeking men

4. Men seeking women

5. Men seeking men

6. Misc. romance

7. Casual encounters

8. Missed connections

9. Rants and raves

The categories are all pretty self-explanatory, but the lines on Craigslist are easily blurred. Men and women both post FWB ads in the "Strictly Platonic" category, and the "women seeking women" section often has ads from couples seeking a bi woman to join the fun.

"Missed connections" is a hodgepodge of people who wished they'd spoken up when they saw a cute guy or gal, but didn't. Here's an example of what you might find here.

Hair by Bonnie

U cut my hair last weekend. You are a gorgeous little thing with a streak of red and pink in your hair. You told me about your plans for the weekend. Get back to me with the style of my haircut if you'd like to be friends with bennies.

That one's pretty typical of this section, or "I saw you when I was cruising through aisles of Walmart Saturday, but couldn't talk because you were with some guys. We smiled a lot every time we crossed paths. If you'd like to meet, tell me what color of coat I was wearing."

Rants and raves are a little more out there. My take is it's just a bunch of crazy people talking shit. It sort of reminds me of Peter Griffin when he hosted "That really grinds my gears…"

Miscellaneous romance is another one off section. A lot of couples use it to try and find a sister wife or slave boy. One lady recently posted she wanted to move in with a couple of gay guys who might be missing a woman's presence around the house. She was willing to cook, clean, and she was even open to joining in with them for oral or anal.

The sections we're going to be using most are:

1) Men seeking women

2) Casual encounters

3) Strictly platonic

These three will pretty much cover any itch you want to have scratched.

The temptation is to always post in "casual encounters," but it's not always the best move. A lot of woman, even if they're looking for some pleasuring, shy away from the casual encounters section. They look at it like going to a bar; they're tired of getting hit on all of the time.

My thought is to play all three categories. A fisherman always has his line in the water; you should too.

Posting a Craigslist ad is easy as can be, and best of all it's free.

Unlike traditional dating sites Craigslist doesn't put you through any hurdles to get started. No personal interest surveys; no questions asking about your body type or what your ideal match should look like; you don't have to give your weight, height, race, age, or any personal information.

On Craigslist you're pretty much anonymous. You can share as much or as little about yourself as you would like to. The only catch is, the more you share, the more responses you're going to get and the better quality they should be.

Like anything else in life, you need to give a little to get a little in return.

If you don't want to tell everyone how old you are, give an age range that you're looking for. If you don't want to tell someone you're fat, tell them you're on the bigger side, or that you resemble Dan Connor. They will get the idea.

If you're looking for someone who's a freak in the sack, say it. If you've always had a fantasy about pounding some chick's hot little ass, put it out there. Or if you're a little shy about putting your innermost fantasies online, you could mention "somewhat kinky a plus." Then you could get into things more when you're emailing back and forth.

The actual mechanics of posting an ad are simple.

Click on the category you want to post your ad in. in the upper right hand part of the page you will see [account] and [post]. If you've never place an ad on Craigslist before select [post]. After this you're given two choices [Log into your account] or [Apply for an account]. Select [apply for an account] and follow the directions.

After your account is set up posting your first ad is easy. Select the category you want to place your ad in; log into your account at the top of the page; and select post. Craigslist will walk you through the basics.

1) **Select a category for your ad**. Most often you're going to choose personal / romance. Then select the sub category – men seeking women, etc.

2) **Write an enticing title**. Give her a reason to click into your ad and find out a little more about you.

3) **Write your ad**. Keep it simple. Be sure to share a little bit about yourself, and then say a few words about what you're looking for. Humor is the best approach. If you can't be funny just say what you have to say like you're talking

to a friend. Normally the more you say, the more real responses you will get.

4) **Add Pictures**. When you're done writing your ad click [continue] at the bottom of the page. This will take you to the next page where you can upload pictures. It's entirely your choice whether you add pictures or not. Click on [Done with pictures] at the bottom of the page.

5) **Publish.** Next you're shown a preview of your ad. If everything looks good click on [Publish] and in a few minutes your ad will be live on Craigslist.

Pat yourself on the back. Sit back, and wait for the responses to come in. Respond to those that have potential.

Find your match. Rinse and repeat as often as you like.

Responding to an ad

The time's going to come when you decide you've just got to respond to an ad you find on Craigslist.

Either you're going come face-to-face with a set of 46 triple D's, or some sexy vixen is going to describe that kinky act you've always wanted to try.

Whether she gets back to you or not depends on how well you respond to her ad.

First thing you need to know, as a guy you're lucky to get five to ten responses to your ad; even the ugliest, fattest, and oldest woman is going to get fifty maybe even one hundred or more responses to their Craigslist ad. That means you're up against some stiff competition every time you respond to an ad. If you want to make the cut you need to step up your game.

The easiest way to do this is to take a look at some individual ads and explain a little bit about how you should respond.

Before we do that I want to talk about the different types of women you're going to find posting ads on Craigslist.

1) Horny housewife. Her husband may be a salesman or trucker and he's on the road all week so she's sitting home alone not getting any.

2) **Revenge sex**. This lady just caught her husband or boyfriend cheating on her and she's looking to get back at him.

3) **Couples**. These folks are looking to add another guy, gal, or couple to their relationship. Most of them will tell you up front what they're looking for. Biggest thing you'll see in every ad – No single men. Best suggestion I can give, read the ad carefully. They will tell you what they want – DP, an extra cock for the wife, sometimes they will both want to work on your cock, and other times she's going to want to watch you do the hubby, or him do you. Before you answer back be sure to know your limits so you can let them know what you will and will not do.

4) **Scratch my itch**. This lady can be a business professional, a busy student, or someone with limited time. She doesn't have time for a real relationship, but she wants someone for some occasional intimate company when she gets the urge. She may be looking for one time or an ongoing thing.

5) **One last time**. She's the older lady, grandma, whatever you want to call her. She's most likely over sixty and is looking for anyone who'll help her out. A lot of the time she manages to hook up with a younger college guy who's going through a dry streak. The good thing is she still has all of the right equipment it just might not be as firm as it used to be.

6) **Big Beautiful Women (BBW's).** These ladies have a little extra meat on their bones, but they easily make up half of the personal ads on most Craigslist sites. They're big ladies with big appetites for sex.

7) **Hooker Bots.** These ads are easy to spot. They either change the s's in their ads to dollar signs; post pictures with their email address across them; or tell you "you've got to pay to play" or "for generous men only." Proceed with caution when you come across one of these ads. It may be a hooker; it may be a police sting.

Ok. Let's take a look at some ads women post and get some ideas about how you should respond to them. Number one tip: Keep that thing in your pants and your camera away from it.

Female wanting male booty

I've always wanted to fuck a guy in the ass. How do you want it – strap-on, dildo, fingers? I won't judge.

Odds are this one is quite real. She's got a fantasy she wants to fulfill. How do you get her in your ass? Tell her why you want to join in the fun? Have you done it before? Is it something you've always fantasized about? Maybe a previous girlfriend shoved her finger up your ass when she was giving you a BJ. The more you can tell her about why you want to do it and what you're expect to get from the experience the better chances you have of being selected.

26 | Banging Your Way Across Craigslist

Getting colder out, need a guy to keep me warm

I'm 33, a BBW (size 16 to 18). I'm single, and not looking for any married or attached guys. I can host, disease free, and 420 friendly. I'm free Friday and Saturday afternoons. I like oral, kissing, cuddling, and touching – no anal. We could meet at a bar down the street from my place, so I can make sure you're not some kind of psycho or axe killer. Once we're clear on that we can head over to my place. Not looking for anything serious, just this weekend. Let's text a little first and we can see where it goes.

This girl's put a lot of thought into it. The cold may have moved her to action, but she's either done this before or thought about it for some time. Focus on her safety. Send a face pic if you're comfortable with it. Stress that you're a normal everyday guy with a career, kids, and ties to the area. Play up the fact that you're clean, tested, and 420 friendly – maybe you could even bring her a little. Let her know you understand her concerns about axe murderers and such; it's a crazy world out there. You may want to hook her up with your Facebook page to prove you're real.

Looking for both of you

I'm very interested in meeting up with a couple at the local adult video store. Does anybody have any info on it? I'm very bisexual, luv having a girl eat my pussy until I squirt all over her face, but I'm also down for a big thick dick. I'm an attractive, bigger lady, and shaved down there. I love eating pussy and sucking dick down on the floor doggie style. Your pics will get mine.

This girl is ready to go. You can bet this isn't her first fuck fest. A massive dick pic may get her attention, but you're not going to get anywhere with her unless you've got another lady you can bring along for the ride. If you're a single guy, don't waste your time trying to change her mind. She's going to have plenty of couples to choose from.

Long term friends with benefits

I'm looking to find a long term fuck buddy, 25 to 35 - absolutely no old guys. You should be single, disease and drug free. I prefer a taller guy, HWP. No tiny dicks, bald dudes, or fat bellies. Send a pick, and tell me why I should fuck you.

Hmm! Look at what she's asking for. Then ask yourself how you stack up. A full body pick (PG) with your face showing is probably important with this one. Go ahead and stress your manly size. If you were just tested, or have any special moves tell her about them.

Pampering

Married and seeking a day off. Looking for a fun filled day; showering me with gifts, soaking in the Jacuzzi, eating a seven course meal in bed at a fine hotel. Let me know what else you have in mind to make my day off really special.

Can you say hooker? Maybe not full on, but all she's looking for is cash and goodies. Totally up to you if you want to pay to play, just keep an eye on your wallet and your drink.

Revenge is a many splendored thing

My boyfriend fucked up and I'm out for some good old fashioned revenge sex. No small wee wee's for this plus sized lady, you're going to need a big dick to take on this big ass.

She's real, and she's looking to get back at that cheating son-of-a-bitch. She included a face and upper body pic, and made it clear she's ready to get it on. Anal play is implied so she's going to be inundated with replies. Get back to her as quick as you can. Include a face and body pick. Let her know how much her situation sucks, and that you've recently been through the same thing. Offer to voice verify or whatever she wants and be sure to stress that you're clean, disease and drug free, and discrete.

BBW fantasy

Larger BBW is looking for someone to help me fulfill my fantasy. I want to fuck two men at the same time. I love sucking cock and want to take two of them in my mouth at once. No women. No anal sex. Just take turns fucking me while I suck the other one off. You must be white and between the ages of 25 and 35. Only contact me if you know someone else who is willing to join in and do this. The only thing that would make it better is if we could take pics, for me only. Let's do it this weekend...

Fantasies are a dude's best friend. The best opportunities to hook up on Craigslist come from helping women fulfill their fantasies – DP, threesomes, anal, gangbangs...

Again read the whole ad carefully. Do you know another guy who will go along with you? Are you comfortable with his junk touching yours? She wants them both in her mouth at the same time so there's no way of keeping them separated. Finally you need to make sure you're the right age, and decide if you're comfortable being filmed in action. If everything is a go get back to her with PG face and body pics of both of you. Play up how cool her fantasy is and how excited you would be to be a part of it.

I want to be filled with a big thick cock

I'm really horny and want to suck on a big fat dick. I'm 5'5 and about 195 lbs., I guess you would call that a smaller BBW. I'm thick, but not obese. You should be thin, attractive, have a big package, and be disease and drug free. Like my dicks trimmed and clean, so send me a pick so I can check out what I'm going to be taking. A face pic would be nice too.

Ok, guys. This is your perfect opportunity to send that dick pick, make sure to clean it up first. Let her know you're totally into BBW's and you have yourself tested regularly. Ask her how she likes it?

All of those ads were taken from the **casual encounters** section. Let's change directions for a few moments and look at some posts from the **women seeking men** section. This is where you're going to get most of your action. There are a lot of young single girls recently out of a relationship that ended badly; older divorces who haven't gotten any for a while; and women who've soured on the results they've gotten from paid dating sites like Cupid and Match.

Are you the one?

I'm looking for a man who knows how to treat a woman, a man who will make her feel special. He should have his act together; have a good job, a car, and a place of his own. Prefer him to be over six foot tall and between 25 and 35.

I'm 5'7" tall, blonde haired, and have a big heart. I'm not the skinniest girl in the world, but I'm not the biggest either. I'm a girly girl, and cuddling is my favorite activity. Summer and fall are my favorite seasons. I enjoy hunting, fishing, camping, and mudding. Nothing beats cuddling up by a bonfire.

Interested? Send me a picture if you can, and tell me something about yourself.

Ok. She's a larger gal. Not the biggest in the world, but... I already told you Craigslist is loaded with BBW's so having a thing for them is a major plus. Her favorite activities are cuddling and bonfires, and she's looking for someone to hold her close. Play up the fact that you're a country guy and enjoy the same things. If you've got a big ass four wheeler you're golden. Be sure to enclose a PG picture and include a longer response to match her posting.

Looking for a mature companion

I'm looking for a mature man. Honesty is a must. You should be between 40 to 50 years old, easy to look at, and fun to be around. I'm a smoker, so you need to be good with that. You should enjoy life, sex, and travel in that order. I can't wait to hear from you.

Her ideal guy should enjoy sex, how convenient is that? Questions to ask yourself before responding to this ad. Are you between the ages of 40 to 50? Are you a smoker, or ok with being around someone who smokes? Do you like to travel? Be sure to hit on all of these points when you respond to her ad. She didn't request a picture, but you should probably include one. She's going to be getting a lot of replies so a good picture could move you closer to the top of her must contact list.

Put a smile on my face

I'm 30 years old, cool as fuck, and am a bigger girl with a few tattoos and piercings. If that's not you're thing, no problem. Just don't go off on me because I'm not a Barbie doll.

I'm looking for someone who will take the time to get to know me, cuddle up on the couch and watch a few movies, and if we get to that point where we make out like teenagers, we can see where it goes. Not sure what I'm looking for. Don't really want to be friends with benefits or some ones fuck buddy.

I'm funny, and I make people laugh a lot. You should too. I don't spend a lot of time in bars and am not looking for anyone who does. Would prefer someone who's a bit nerdy, and can carry on a good conversation

Let me know.

She's cool as fuck. Just ask her and she will tell you so. She's not really looking for a fuck buddy, but passionate kissing and cuddling is an option so you're a good deal of the way there. You should include a detailed reply. Stress that you're into bigger girls; you're somewhat of a nerd, and read a lot on just about every subject; you're not sure what you're looking for right now. You're just looking to make a new friend and see where it goes. You might want to mention you weren't the class clown back in school but you ran a close second.

Baby it's cold outside...

I've been looking for the real thing but keep drawing a blank. I'm an older gal looking for that special guy to spend my time with, and see where it goes. I'm clean, attractive, disease and drug free. I'm not looking for a sugar daddy and don't expect to be your sugar momma. You should have time available for a relationship and enjoy doing things together. I am looking for a younger man, and I do enjoy sex. You should be under 35, attractive, and know how to treat a lady.

She's looking for a younger guy, under age 35, and she enjoys sex. Everything is looking good so far. She doesn't want to support you; she doesn't expect you to support her either, so she's not gunning for your money. She's older, but we don't know how old. She wants a younger guy under 35, so we can assume she's somewhere in her late 40's or early 50's, maybe even her early sixties. Send her a short response about how you've always had this thing for older ladies. Let her know you're attractive, not attached to your job so you have time for a relationship, and you're open to whatever she's up for. Don't bring up sex, let her do that in her reply, and pace your response to match what she has to say.

It's too cold to sleep alone

I'm single and happy with it but am growing tired of sleeping alone. I'm at a point where I want someone to cuddle and sleep with on a regular basis, after we have some crazy sex of course, that's just part of getting to know each other. I don't want to play any games. You need to be available, easily to look at, at able to use it more than once in a night.

I'm a BBW, fat, chubby, whatever you want to call it. Some guys would say I'm not too hard on your eyes. Should be close to my age (39), live within ten miles of me or be willing to haul your ass over here whenever we get the urge, and willing to share a few pictures.

If any of this sounds like it might be you hit me up with a few pictures (no dick pics), and say more than "What's up!" or I'll delete your response, no matter what you look like.

Sex is a given with this gal. Are you're looking for a regular thing? She's a bigger gal, been alone for a while, and wants to get freaky in the sack. How do you approach her? Talk about the weather. "I know what you're talking about. All of this cold is making me wish I had a warm soft body to wrap my arms around and help me keep warm. It's been a while and I know what you mean about sleeping alone." After that tell her a little bit about yourself, maybe just one freaky sexual adventure you've had or always wanted to have, and whatever you do – Play up the fact that BBW's are your thing.

Single BBW for casual...maybe more

I'm a single white BBW, age 45. I'm looking for an ongoing thing – dinner or lunch, movies, concert, and of course regular adult activities as long as you don't have any freaky or strange fetishes. You should be close to my age, able to carry on a conversation (without constantly checking your phone), and able to pay your own way. I'm not looking for any free loaders; I've got my own bills to pay. Convince me you're a real person, and not some Craigslist troll.

Right off, you know she's done this before when she talks about Craigslist trolls. Best way to approach her is to keep it casual, and share whatever info you're comfortable giving out. Don't go crazy and give her your social security or credit card numbers, but it wouldn't hurt to send a few pictures of your standing by your house or car. That will take away those freeloader worries. Other than that convince her you're an ordinary guy. Tell her you've got a job, a place to live, and kids. You're not some kind of freak, and the closest your ever came to BDSM was when you got your arm all tangled up in a previous girl friends bra.

Hopefully that gives you an idea how to respond to the different types of ads you're going to come across.

The majority of unattached women on Craigslist are BBW's. Hopefully you like your ladies with a little meat on them or can acquire a taste for them.

Keep in mind a lot of the women on Craigslist are attached and looking for playmates to join their relationships. Sometimes hubby will want to join in, other times they get off watching the wife get nailed.

The key takeaways are:

1) Keep running new ads. Experiment with different ads, and place them in different categories.

2) When you respond to an ad, pace yourself to the length and tone set in the ad. If she's humorous, send a humorous reply; if she's serious make a more thoughtful response.

3) Keep that thing in your pants and keep your camera away from it. Don't send a dick pick unless she asks for it.

Keep your responses fun and casual. Craigslist is a fun site and you're going to meet a lot of interesting people during the time you spend on it.

Not all of your experiences will be pleasant, but overall the good should outweigh the bad.

If you're a "cup is half empty type of guy," you're going to be pissed off because no one is responding to your ads; you're going to be sure there's no real girls on Craigslist. You're going to tell everybody there's just a bunch of fat ugly chicks and hookers there.

If you're a "cup is half full type of guy," you're going to love every minute of it. What could be better than meeting new women every day, and being chased by women rather than the other way around.

Remember, life is all about how you approach it.

Sample ads

Writing your ad is actually half the fun of Craigslist dating.

If you've taken any time to look through the postings there you know the writing is subpar, littered with misspellings and totally atrocious grammar. What would the Grammar Girl think?

My suggestion is to double and triple check your ads before you post them. Clean up all of those annoying typos; don't use abbreviations that no one understands; and eliminate the urge to run everything together. Try to include a number of short paragraphs. Use a variety of short and long sentences. Most importantly read the ad a few times before you post it. Does it say what you want it to? Does it mention what you want her to include in her reply? If so, then you're ready to let her rip.

The first few sample ads are pretty generic. They're longer than most of the postings you're going to find on Craigslist. They don't come right out and ask for sex, you're both adults, and can work that out later if the chemistry is right.

Baby step your way to success. I've tried hundreds of different approaches with my Craigslist ads, and longer non-threatening ads draw the most responses. The natural urge is to ask for a picture up front. The longer you can keep from requesting a picture the better the conversation you're going to have.

What should you talk about? Write your ad like you would approach a letter to a friend. Talk about the things you like to do. Toss in a few details about what makes it so fun. Is there something you'd like to do but not having a partner there to experience it with you holds you back? Ask her to do it with you. "I always wanted to go parachuting, but I'm afraid to take the plunge on my own. None of my friends will do it, will you?"

"The new Sandra Bullock movie comes out this weekend and the guys say it's too gay for them to go see with me. Any ladies out there like to see it with me?"

Do you see how easy it is?

A great personal ad should be a conversation starter. Say a little bit about yourself or what you'd like to do, then ask her if she'd like to join you.

If you're the kind of guy who just has to work sex into the first line of your ad approach it the same way. Don't say "want to fuck?" or "suck on this." Tell her what you like about sex; how it makes you feel; or some kinky fantasy you've always wanted to try but you never had anybody to do it with.

Tired of sitting home alone

Here I am sitting home alone – again. I'm looking for a lady age 32 to 55 who might want to stop by for the afternoon. We could grab some snacks watch a little TV, or just talk. It could be a regular thing. If something more develops - great, if not, at least we made a new friend and spent a few afternoons together.

I'm in my mid-fifties, not too horrible to look at, and would like to meet someone fun to talk to and hang out with.

Send me a pic and tell me a little bit about yourself.

Days are getting longer and colder

Days are getting longer and colder, I'm looking for a soft warm cuddle buddy to heat up my nights.

Could you be her? I'm looking for a gal to come over, cuddle up close on the couch and watch a few movies. Nothing too serious, just good talk, fun... and if it warms up outside maybe we could grab a bite, or catch a movie now and then.

Tell me what you'd like to watch and I'll have snacks and wine waiting for you.

I can't wait to hear from you. Be sure to tell me a little bit about yourself, one line responses are so impersonal.

I'm willing to lie about how we met

Here's the deal. I'm a bigger guy (You know what that means –fat!) I don't drink, do drugs, or go to bars, so that really limits my chances of meeting new people. I do like to eat out now and then, and going to a movie could be fun. I spend a lot of time at home watching TV and reading. When it's warmer I like to sit on the deck and watch the world pass by.

Local road trips would be nice if I had a companion, so would an overnighter to Chicago. I will warn you I'm a meat and potatoes type of guy, so no fancy restaurants or gourmet joints. I prefer jeans to suits. I can be funny, sometimes to the point of being rude or sarcastic (Sorry! That's just me being me).

Kurt Vonnegut readers move to the front of the line. It you've ever read John Kennedy Toole add two bonus points in your favor.

If you want to stop by and watch some TV, or just talk, that would be great. Or we could meet at a restaurant, grab a burger and fries, and see where it goes. Who knows –

Maybe we could be the next Bogie and Bacall, maybe just friends. Who knows – we might even just walk away.

At least we tried.

If you're feeling bold shoot me a picture and a few words about yourself, I'll return the favor. Size, age, race doesn't really matter. I would prefer someone between ages 35 and 55, but am open to others if you feel there's a compelling reason we should meet.

PS: I have an open time spot this Friday if you want to meet me on the couch. We could watch a little TV, swap secrets, or make fun of people we don't even know (that always makes me smile).

I can't wait to hear from you.

Friends, Friends with benefits...

Friends, friends with benefits, or anything else you want to call it. Lonely guy here looking to spend some time with a gal who finds herself in a similar situation.

I normally like my ladies with a little meat on their bones, but if you look like Marilyn Monroe or a young Raquel Welch (circa One Million BC); what the hell! I might just be willing to take a chance on you.

Just so you know I'm more the Dan Connor type. Rosanne flew the coop so I'm auditioning for her replacement.

Anyway, if you'd care to take a chance and see if something sparks between us, hit me up with a few lines about yourself, and what you're looking for.

Holidays are a great time to inject some humor into your message. The ads you write should be fun to read and loaded with off the wall humor. You're going to get some really great responses. I find the crazier my ad is the more insane the responses I'll get. They generate a lot of quick one-liners where you can just play around, get comfortable, and easily move into exchanging more intimate details as the conversation moves on.

You can use these sample ads, adapt them to something that reflects your personality, or come up with something totally unique.

The Big day is over and Santa's feeling a little lonely.

The presents have all been delivered. The sleigh has been parked; the reindeer unhitched; and the elves are all off for a good days rest. When I walked into the house what should I find but a letter from Mrs. Claus. She ran off with an elf; it seems her Christmas wish was for one wild fling. Now Santa's feeling a little lonely and is looking for his own little elf.

No need to say much about my looks. You all know about my big belly full of jelly. A word of warning though, I always wear red, right down to my skivvies; so if that color sets you off you better move on.

I've got some personality quirks you may find particularly disturbing. I'm always dishing out presents; the elves keep bursting into the house at all hours with ideas for the latest, greatest toys ever; and the reindeers. Some of the things they do in the house. Well, you can smell it for days. Rudolph's getting on in years now and you'll often find him wearing a low hanging diaper. Mrs. Claus used to care for that, hopefully you're somewhat good with pins and diaper cloths?

If I haven't discouraged you yet and you can make it here through this cold snowy night, are there any ladies up to the task of making this old fellow jolly.

And though I've said it many times – Ho! Ho! Ho! Santa's not about to pay, so if that's your deal just so you know you'll make the naughty list right quick should you try.

Merry Christmas to all, and to all a good night!

Bah – Hum-Bug! Looking for my Christmas Cheer

Not saying I'm Mr. Scrooge or anything like that, but here I am sitting home all alone on Christmas Eve. I've got plenty of coal to keep the fire going all night; the couch is warm, the TV's blaring; and the Christmas feast is waiting by the table.

The only thing missing is – you. Care to brighten up the Holiday for this Christmas Grinch. I'm already mixing movies which can only mean one thing – too many drinks for me and not enough for you.

Mr. Scrooge is looking for Mrs. Marley – Could you be her?

The weather is another great conversation starter. Everybody bitches about the weather. "It's too fucking cold out the there." When's this freaking rain going to stop?" "Weatherman says it's the hottest summer on record."

Everybody talks about the weather. I used to be a telemarketer and one of the easiest ways to build rapport with a customer was to ask,

"How's the weather in Texas? You weren't affected by the recent ice storms were you?"

"No, but two counties over everything stopped dead. There were wrecks everywhere."

"Doesn't sound fun at all. I'm up here in Iowa and it is cold as can be. It's 20 below zero outside, but no snow or ice."

Believe it or not, Craigslist works the same way. Talk about the weather, and women are going to talk back.

We recently had a week long streak of cold weather with the wind chills dipping down below -50° for a couple of days. That brought out the nastiness in me and these ads reflect that.

Brrr! It's fucking cold out there...

I'm tired of this freaking cold, any ladies out there up to braving the cold. Maybe you could stop over and help me warm things up a bit?

Don't wait too long though, or I may have to give myself a hand.

What's that you say? Schools cancelled for a snow day.

Just because schools been cancelled and the kids are staying home for the day doesn't mean mom should be punished too. If you can slip away for a few hours, I've got a warm fire roaring, the Walking Dead is on TV, and I could crack the cap on a bottle of wine or a few long tops.

Drop me a few lines about why mom deserves a snow day, and the things she'd like to do with me.

Sometimes you've just got to say it. Come on, scream it out with me, "I want it, and I want it now!"

I've already said asking for sex up front is the kiss of death in most case, but not always. It sometimes depends on how you make your case.

A lot of people, both men and women, make their way towards Craigslist because they've got something really kinky or crazy they want to try out. Many times it's some deep dark fantasy they've been harboring for years. They're afraid to share it with a spouse or lover, but maybe they could do it with a stranger.

How about you? What's your deepest, darkest fantasy that you've never shared with anyone?

Let me tell you about a few of them I've seen on Craigslist over the years.

There's knotting. That was a new one, even for me, and I admit I had to look it up in the urban dictionary. It seems some people like to do it with our doggie friends, and other folks just like to watch.

A lot of people are just looking for someone to hang out naked with – other guys, other gals, or couples. They don't really want to have sex. They just want to let it all hang out. Some couples need a place to do it, and if you can provide it they'll let you watch, or maybe even join in. Some folks are interested in watersports, and others are more curious about what comes out the other end.

I've seen a lot of guys and gals seeking their personal slaves – sex and otherwise. Twice I've come across ads for guys wanting their women to prance around in diapers. They couldn't wait to watch the young lady soil her diaper.

Many of the requests are more vanilla than that. A lot of couples are looking to spice things up by adding a guy or a gal to their lovemaking. Some gals are looking for two guys to have a DP fuck fest, and of course, you will even find a few dungeon masters.

Pick your fantasy and put it out there. Keep posting once or twice a week; eventually you should find some takers.

Final wrap up

Craigslist dating is a lifestyle choice. If you don't watch it it can easily become an obsession like Facebook where you have to check back every few moments to scope out the newest post.

Some guys have a lot of success hooking up on Craigslist, you'll hear other say it's a total waste of time. They say it's nothing but a bunch of hooker bots, fat ugly chicks, and druggies.

What they're missing is that like anything else, it's all about how you approach it. If you post a bunch of lame ass ads, and don't hear back from any real ladies, there's a reason for it. If you take the time to really work it.

If you craft original ads women can relate to that make you come across as a real person, real women will respond to you.

How do you do that?

Obviously, you don't shout out "Hey, any ladies WANT TO FUCK!" You've got to work on developing unique approaches that make you appear like someone she would be interested in meeting with. You need to make her laugh. You need to make her take notice and understand that you're the kind of guy she'd be crazy not to want to know better.

In short, it's just like going to the pickup bar. If you're approaching her with a bunch of cheesy one-liners you're not going to make the cut.

If you decide you've just got to post a dick pick in every ad you're not going to get the opportunity to whip it out in front of a real lady.

Best advice I can give you.

1) **Be genuine**. Let her see that you're a real person and have an understanding of what real relationships are all about.

2) **Be spontaneous and funny**. Humor is probably the best icebreaker out there. Go back to my burger basket ad. All of the girls had a great time responding to my big spender habits in that one. It gave us a good opportunity to banter one-liners back and forth, and just be playful for a while. Consider it your warm up. The longer you can keep her engaged in small talk the closer you are to meeting up.

3) **Don't be a sore loser**. A lot of conversations on Craigslist just stop. Many times it looks really good, and when you go to exchange pictures, the conversation just drops and you never hear back. Same thing goes when it's time to set up the meet and greet. It's the actual moment of truth and you lose a lot of people here. They were in love with the idea of meeting someone new, but when it comes time to meet – they just can't move past that fear. Understand that it's going to happen – a lot. Accept it, and be ready to move on.

4) **Be yourself**. Life's too short to pretend you're someone else. If a girls doesn't like you for who you are; run another ad and find someone who will.

Whatever you do – don't give up. Whether you're looking for a string of one night stands where you can sample all of the local cuisine; looking to find an ongoing friend with bennies; or true love – You will find it if you keep pushing forward.

I'm proof that you really can bang your way across Craigslist.